W9-CHG-698

IN THE ZONE

SCUBA DIVING

DAVID HUNTRODS

MEDIA ENHANCED BOOKS
AV2 BY WEIGL
ADDED VALUE · AUDIO VISUAL

www.av2books.com

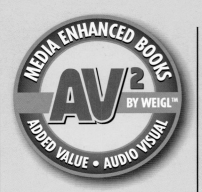

AV² provides enriched content that supplements and complements this book. Weigl's AV² books strive to create inspired learning and engage young minds in a total learning experience.

Your AV² Media Enhanced books come alive with...

Audio
Listen to sections of the book read aloud.

Key Words
Study vocabulary, and complete a matching word activity.

Video
Watch informative video clips.

Quizzes
Test your knowledge.

Go to **www.av2books.com**, and enter this book's unique code.

Embedded Weblinks
Gain additional information for research.

Slide Show
View images and captions, and prepare a presentation.

BOOK CODE

B 2 3 3 1 6 2

AV² by Weigl brings you media enhanced books that support active learning.

Try This!
Complete activities and hands-on experiments.

... and much, much more!

Download the AV² catalog at **www.av2books.com/catalog**

AV² Online Navigation on page 24

Published by AV² by Weigl
350 5th Avenue, 59th Floor
New York, NY 10118
Website: www.av2books.com   www.weigl.com

Library of Congress Cataloging-in-Publication Data
Huntrods, David.
Scuba diving / David Huntrods.
    p. cm. -- (In the zone)
Includes index.
Summary: "Provides information about the fundamentals of scuba, from equipment and moves to superstars and legends. Intended for third to fifth grade students"--Provided by publisher.
ISBN 978-1-62127-320-2 (hardcover : alk. paper) -- ISBN 978-1-62127-325-7 (softcover : alk. paper)
1. Scuba diving--Juvenile literature. I. Title.
GV838.672.H86 2013
797.2'34--dc23

                          2012043984

Printed in the United States in North Mankato, Minnesota
1 2 3 4 5 6 7 8 9 0 17 16 15 14 13

012013
WEP301112

PROJECT COORDINATOR Aaron Carr
EDITOR Steve Macleod
ART DIRECTOR Terry Paulhus

Every reasonable effort has been made to trace ownership and to obtain permission to reprint copyright material. The publishers would be pleased to have any errors or omissions brought to their attention so that they may be corrected in subsequent printings.

Weigl acknowledges Getty Images as its primary image supplier for this title.

IN THE ZONE

CONTENTS

■ Scuba diving opened up an exciting new underwater world for people to explore.

Scuba stands for "self-contained underwater breathing apparatus." One of the first scuba devices was made in England. That was in 1825. Navy forces around the world began making scuba equipment. They used it to explore underwater. They also used scuba equipment for ship repairs. The United States Navy created a diving helmet in 1917. It was used until 1980.

■ Scuba is an **acronym.** It was written for many years in all capital letters. Scuba is now so common that it is an ordinary word and no longer needs to be written with all capital letters.

Divers tried other ways to breathe before scuba equipment. The diving bell was invented in 1535. It was a metal bell full of air. It would be lowered into the water. Divers swam inside the bell when they needed to breathe. People also used diving suits. They were connected to a ship by a hose. The diver would breathe through the hose.

Early scuba systems were called **rebreathers.** One was the Momsen Lung. It was invented by Charles "Swede" Momsen. He was in the United States Navy. The Momsen Lung was a small rubber bag filled with air. Air from the diver would be recycled in the bag. Then the diver could breathe the air again. Jacques Yves Cousteau and Emile Gagnan invented the Aqua Lung in 1943. It was a tank with **compressed air** inside. This allowed divers to breathe underwater for a long time.

People were able to explore underwater. Scuba diving soon became popular. Small diving clubs began teaching scuba courses. Today, scuba diving is more popular than ever.

S cuba divers wear a tank full of air. This helps them breathe underwater. The tank is a metal cylinder. It has a valve on top. The air in the tank is under high **pressure**. This allows the tank to hold a lot of air in a small space.

The body suit is made of rubber or stretchy plastic. It covers the whole body. The suit protects the diver from scrapes, cuts, and from the cold.

Divers have a **regulator** to breathe the air inside the tank. It is connected to the tank's air valve by a hose. This valve allows air to flow through the regulator when the diver breathes in, but stops the air when the diver breathes out.

The amount of air someone needs depends on how deep he or she dives. More air is needed for a deep dive. A dive computer tracks how deep the diver is underwater. It also keeps track of how much air the diver has left.

■ The vest holds the tank in place. It can also fill with air to raise the diver to the surface. This special dive vest is called a Buoyancy Control Device (BCD). Weights can be added to the BCD to keep the diver balanced in the water.

■ Flippers are long rubber fins that fit over the feet. With fins, a diver can swim more quickly underwater.

■ The mask is a small window of glass that seals around the eyes and nose. It allows a diver to see clearly underwater. A **snorkel** may be attached to the mask for breathing near the surface.

Scuba divers can explore colorful reefs. Reefs are formations made of limestone. They form in shallow water. Reefs grow over millions of years. The Great Barrier Reef is off the coast of Australia. It is 1,243 miles (2,000 kilometers) long. It is the largest coral reef system in the world.

Reefs are found in warmer water. They are home to many tropical fish and other sea life. The Florida Keys has a coral reef system divers can explore. The reef has different **marine** life, such as turtles and sharks. There are also different types of coral.

■ Scuba diving gives people a chance to come face to face with fascinating underwater animals in their natural habitat.

Shipwrecks are also popular dive sites. There are many ships and airplanes that have sunk to the ocean floor. Many of these wrecks are now home to sea life. Scuba diving allows people to explore these wrecks. They can also provide a lesson in history.

The *USS Indra* is a popular shipwreck. The Indra was built in the United States in 1945. The ship was taken out of service in 1989. It was sunk on purpose off the coast of North Carolina. The state's government wanted to create a reef. Divers can now explore the ship.

■ Shipwrecks offer divers a chance to explore underwater. Divers are sometimes able to find valuable items in the wrecks.

Being underwater can be dangerous. Divers must be careful. They must make a plan before they dive. Divers should know how much air is in their tanks, how deep they can go, and how long they can stay underwater. A diver should always plan to use less air than what is available in the tank.

Divers should always check their equipment before they enter the water. They do not want problems with it when they are underwater.

As divers swim deeper, there is more pressure on their bodies. The space for air in their lungs becomes smaller and the air gets heavier. Swimming up or down too quickly can be dangerous. Scuba equipment will adjust to changes in pressure, but divers must remember to breathe normally. New divers should not swim too deep. Swimming at a proper depth reduces the need for **decompression**.

■ An instructor or guide will let a diver know how deep they can go and remain safe.

Divers should only dive at sites that are safe for their level of training and experience. They should be aware of any risks at the site. They should find out about dangerous marine life or strong currents. It is best to dive with a professional guide or instructor. These experts will be able to handle any danger.

It is important for divers to use a **buddy system**. Dive buddies keep an eye on their partner at all times. They watch for problems or signs of sickness. A dive buddy helps out in case of an emergency.

Divers always keep a dive log. In a dive log, they record details of where, how long, and how deep they have dived. Divers also show their dive log to prove their experience level when diving at a new place.

■ Underwater cages can protect divers when exploring sites with sharks.

Scuba diving can be fun, but there are many things to know in order to dive safely. Divers must be certified before they dive. To become certified, a diver takes a course, does practice dives, and passes a test. There are many different levels of certification. The basic level is a **recreational dive** certificate. It is sometimes called an "open water" certificate.

■ Shipwreck diving courses show divers how to avoid snagging their equipment when going through tight spaces.

There are other types of certifications. Divers can train for certain types of dive sites and equipment. There is special wreck diving certification. This course teaches divers how to explore inside a shipwreck without getting lost. Some other special certifications include: cave diving, night diving, and training to use underwater scooters.

Divers should be strong swimmers. Divers should have a certificate to show their swimming level. As well, first aid courses and **CPR training** are valuable for scuba divers.

■ Most scientists who perform underwater research have scuba diving certification.

■ In an emergency, dive buddies can share air by passing one regulator back and forth.

S cuba groups are different from most sport leagues. They do not focus on competing. Instead, they provide training and opportunities to dive. The two largest scuba diving groups are the Professional Association of Diving Instructors (PADI) and the National Association of Underwater Instructors (NAUI).

Most early diving groups focused on professional divers, but PADI was different. In 1966, PADI began to offer scuba training to both **amateur** and professional divers. This allowed more people to try scuba. In this way, PADI helped launch recreational diving as a popular sport around the world.

PADI offers courses from beginner to advanced levels. Divers can move up the levels by passing training courses. These courses test a diver's knowledge and ability in scuba. A diver must complete many dives before he or she can take higher-level courses. Getting that far takes practice and hard work.

■ Diving clubs across the country provide people with an opportunity to try scuba diving.

NAUI is mostly for serious sport divers and professionals. It was founded in Los Angeles County in 1959. It was one of the first major diving groups. Jacques Cousteau was one of its members.

NAUI is a worldwide organization. Their courses are more difficult than courses in PADI. NAUI teaches different divers, from **search and rescue divers** to professional **salvage divers**, how to do their work safely.

■ Scuba training can be held in a swimming pool until divers are experienced enough for the ocean.

Scuba has attracted people of all ages. Television programs and movies of undersea life have made scuba more popular than ever before.

Hans Hass

CAREER FACTS:

- Hass was born in Austria in 1919. He was a pioneer in underwater photography.
- He gave speeches, wrote books, and produced movies about underwater life. One of his movies won first prize for major **documentaries** at the Venice Bienniele film festival in 1951.
- In 1998, Hass was honored by The Academy of Underwater Arts and Sciences for pioneering marine exploration and research.
- He is a member of the International Scuba Divers Hall of Fame.

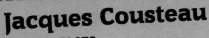

Jacques Cousteau

CAREER FACTS:

- In 1950, Cousteau purchased an English Navy mine-sweeper and converted it into a floating laboratory for undersea research.
- He produced more than 120 documentaries about the undersea world. Three of those films won Academy Awards.
- Cousteau helped increase the popularity of scuba around the world with his television series, *The Undersea World of Jacques Cousteau.*
- Cousteau was awarded the United States Presidential Medal of Freedom in 1985 and he was honored with membership in the French Academy in 1989.

Zale Parry

CAREER FACTS:

- Parry began scuba diving in 1951. She was one of the first female professional scuba divers.
- In 1960, Parry became the first female president of the Underwater Photographic Society. She helped organize the first International Underwater Film Festival.
- In 2002, she was inducted into the Cayman Island International Scuba Diving Hall of Fame and received the Beneath the Sea Diver of the Year Award.
- In 2006, The Academy of Underwater Arts and Sciences began awarding an annual scholarship in Parry's name to young people seeking careers in ocean exploration, research, and conservation.

Ben Cropp

CAREER FACTS:

- Cropp has produced more than 150 marine and wildlife documentaries.
- In 1964, he was named Underwater Photographer of the Year.
- In 1977, Cropp discovered *The Pandora*, Australia's most important shipwreck.
- In 2000, he was inducted into the International Scuba Divers Hall of Fame.

Some scientists and photographers use scuba in their work. Scuba is also a recreational sport for people who like to view undersea life.

Gary Gentile

CAREER FACTS:

- Gentile is a pioneer of wreck diving and is an expert on underwater recovery.
- In 1989, he won the right for divers to explore important shipwrecks such as the *USS Monitor*.
- He has published 58 books, more than 3,000 photographs, and discovered more than 40 shipwrecks.
- Gentile wrote the first handbook on technical diving.

Greg Mossfeldt

CAREER FACTS:

- Mossfeldt has been diving since 1989.
- He has worked as an underwater photographer, exploring several famous shipwrecks.
- He filmed underwater footage for television documentaries, such as *Doomed Sisters of the Titanic* in 1999 and *Hitler's Lost U-boat* in 2000.
- Mossfeldt's library of underwater film footage has been used to promote interest in diving across North America.

Howard and Michele Hall

CAREER FACTS:

- Howard and Michele have directed and produced four underwater IMAX films.
- Howard and Michele have also directed and produced television series for National Geographic and PBS.
- Howard and Michele have won seven Emmy Awards for their work.
- They were inducted into the International Scuba Diving Hall of Fame in 2011.

Dr. Sylvia Earle

CAREER FACTS:

- Earle is an **oceanographer** with the National Geographic Society.
- She was named "hero of the planet" by *Time* magazine in 1998.
- She has led more than 100 expeditions and logged nearly 7,000 hours underwater.
- Earle has written several books about oceans and undersea life for both adults and children.

Scuba divers must be healthy and fit. Breathing and swimming underwater is hard work. Proper eating and exercise are very important to prepare for an enjoyable scuba dive. Scuba divers should eat a balanced diet that includes all the major food groups. Eating balanced meals helps athletes work harder for longer periods of time.

■ Athletes need to drink fluids before, during, and after exercising.

■ It is important to eat 5 to 9 servings of vegetables a day.

Scuba equipment is easy to manage in the water. However, divers must also carry their equipment to the dive site. Out of the water, scuba tanks, suits, and other equipment are heavy and bulky. Divers should stretch and warm up before heading to the dive site.

Exercising several times a week builds strength and **endurance** for diving. Swimming is one of the best forms of exercise for scuba divers. It exercises the whole body, including the heart and lungs. A healthy heart is important for scuba diving.

■ Stretching and breathing exercises improves the body's flexibility and strength. This helps prevent injuries and strains when carrying scuba equipment.

Test your scuba knowledge by trying to answer these brain teasers!

1 What does SCUBA mean?

2 What equipment does a person need to go scuba diving?

3 In what year was the Aqua Lung invented?

4 What do divers write in their dive log?

5 What is the largest coral reef system in the world?

6 What organization helped make diving a popular recreational sport?

ANSWERS: 1. SCUBA stands for "self-contained underwater breathing apparatus." 2. A diver needs a tank, a regulator, a dive computer, a diving suit and vest, a mask, and flippers. 3. 1943. 4. They write information about each dive, such as where, how long, and how deep they dived. 5. The Great Barrier Reef. 6. The Professional Association of Diving Instructors (PADI).

Key Words

acronym: a word formed from the first letter of each word in a series of words

amateur: a person who does something for fun, rather than for pay

buddy system: a system in which a person always dives with a partner

compressed air: air that is under a lot of pressure

CPR training: a course about how to help a person whose heart is not beating and who has stopped breathing

decompression: rest stops made when coming to the surface after a dive

documentaries: fact-based programs

endurance: the ability to work or exercise for a long time

marine: having to do with the sea

oceanographer: a scientist who studies oceans and undersea life

pressure: a physical force pressing against something

rebreathers: a scuba system that uses filters to make air breathable again

recreational dive: a type of diving done just for fun

regulator: a special mouthpiece that controls the air supply from a diver's tank; it shuts off air flow when the diver does not need it

salvage divers: divers who recover useful items or material from sunken vessels

search and rescue divers: divers who search for and rescue people in trouble in the water

snorkel: a short tube that a swimmer uses for breathing just below the surface of the water

Index

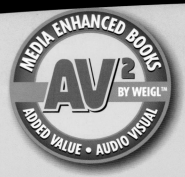

Log on to www.av2books.com

AV² by Weigl brings you media enhanced books that support active learning. Go to www.av2books.com, and enter the special code found on page 2 of this book. You will gain access to enriched and enhanced content that supplements and complements this book. Content includes video, audio, weblinks, quizzes, a slide show, and activities.

AV² Online Navigation

Book Pages
AV² pages directly correspond to pages in the book.

Audio
Listen to sect... the book rea...

Video
Watch inform... video clips.

Embedded Web...
Gain additional informa... for research.

Key Words
Study vocabulary, and complete a matching word activity.

Quizzes
Test your knowledge.

Slide Show
View images and captions, and prepare a presentation.

Try This!
Complete activities and hands-on experiments.

AV² was built to bridge the gap between print and digital. We encourage you to tell us what you like and what you want to see in the future.

Sign up to be an AV² Ambassador at www.av2books.com/ambassador.